Smyth & Helwys Publishing, Inc.
6316 Peake Road
Macon, Georgia 31210-3960
1-800-747-3016
©2019 by Ragan Courtney

Library of Congress Cataloging-in-Publication Data

Names: Courtney, Ragan, author.
Title: Do you still do things with clay? / by Ragan Courtney.
Description: Macon, GA : Smyth & Helwys Publishing, 2019.
Identifiers: LCCN 2018056822 | ISBN 9781641731041 (paperback : alk. paper)
Subjects: LCSH: Christian poetry, American--21st century. | American
poetry--21st century.
Classification: LCC PS3553.O862 A6 2019 | DDC 811/.54--dc23
LC record available at https://lccn.loc.gov/2018056822

Do You Still Do Things with Clay?

RAGAN COURTNEY

Also by Ragan Courtney

Poems

Meditations for the Suddenly Single

The Wind I Soar On

Death Has Set My Mind on Fire

Three Voices

Holy Ghosts

Shall the clay say to him who forms it,
"What are you making?"
—YAHWEH
(Isaiah 45:9)

Dedication

This book is dedicated to Professor Ivey Gravette, a teacher who influenced my life profoundly. She walked down the tiled floor of Alexandria Hall at Louisiana College in Pineville with determination. Her low leather heels clicked a staccato message into my anxious heart. I was anxious because I had been warned to avoid her classes at any cost, for she was an exacting teacher and very demanding of her students. With that warning, the sound of her heels on the floor resonated like bullets being fired as this gorgon of a teacher approached the classroom. She had already retired once. I seriously doubt it was the magnetism of the students that had her extending her tenure. Perhaps it was a financial reason or simply the love of teaching a subject about which she felt passionately that called her back to this small liberal arts school. Whatever the reason, in the scheme of my life and eternity, I was fortunate to fall under her tutelage. She carried her books across her chest, like any co-ed would, casually tossed her sweater across the back of her chair, smiled at us, totally disarming me, and said, "Wordsworth was a great poet!" Little did I know, but those words, that simple sentence, would change my life.

She was a teacher who expected her students to do outside readings and gave us daily assignments. It never crossed my mind not to read her assignments, and I read with relish. I read for two primary reasons, I think. One, I was delighted with the new knowledge. Two, I wanted to impress Professor Gravette. That need to impress her caused me to be one of the first students to raise my hand when she asked the same question every day with the same inflection: "What have you gleaned from your outside readings?" The word "gleaned" seemed to be sung, as she elongated the vowel, saying/singing, "gle-e-e-e-aned." I don't remember verbatim the conversations we had in class, but I do remember that we conversed. Today I find myself wondering if the fact that she created a space for conversation was how I really learned. It was not the readings themselves but the free exchange of ideas that inspired me and encouraged my desire for such communication throughout my life.

She has been gone for many years now, but her life force remains with me to this day when I read Emily Dickinson, William Wordsworth, Samuel Coleridge, John Keats, Pablo Neruda, Robert Frost, Walt Whitman, Mary

Oliver, Wendell Berry, Rainer Maria Rilke, Hafiz, Billy Collins, or any number of poets—it is a long list. I wish she were here with me even now so I could ask her about this thought or that meter, this metaphor or that rhyme. She taught passionately about beauty and truth. If that makes her sound like a saint, she was.

Contents

Preface 1

Prayer #999 3

The World Is Spiritually Hungry 4

The Way the Words Fall from My Mouth 5

Idle Wish 7

Weavings 8

The Calling 11

Set in Stone 14

I Read Poets and Prophets 15

Sweet Vengeance 18

Louder 19

Revive Us Again 21

Hawkers and Mockers 22

Pearl of Great Price 25

To a Young Theologian 26

The Cross Is Protestant Bare 29

Cain's Markings 31

They Shall See God 33

Them and Us 36

Lines of People 38

White Flags 40

Inner Wars 41

Our Vantage Point 43

Apocalypse 45

Waiting 48

Hope Is Everywhere 50

Angels Dancing 51

The Old, Wise Ones 53

Heart Song 55

I Sit Still 56

Annunciation 57

Keeping X in Xmas 59

Betrayer 61

Corpus Christi 63

Hunger and Thirst 65
Burning Mystery 67
Thoughts on Seeing for the First Time 69
The Passion of St. Genesius 72
La Posada 78
It's the Simple Things that Get You 79
The Wall 80
Heroic Feelings. 82
Voyage 84
The Story of the Antediluvian World 85
    Before. 85
    Shame 89
    After. 89
Labyrinth 93
Santa Fe Afternoon. 96
New Mexican Monsoon 97
From Whence the Gods 98
The Psalms. 100
    A Clean Heart 100
    Upright 102
    Calm the Waters, Lord. 104
    Liturgy. 106
    Show Us God 108
    Dominion? 109
    Autumnal Days. 110
Prayer. 112
The Bread of Life 115
When Paradise 117
Souvenir. 119
With Thanks to Rilke. 124
Take, Eat 126
Star Stuff 128
The Bride of Christ 130
Meditations 132
Dawn at Madeline's 133
Fired Clay Cup. 134
Addendum: A Little Child Shall Lead Them 135

Preface

The day that I found myself standing in the pulpit of a church, preaching a sermon as the newly called pastor of a small congregation in Austin, Texas, was terrifying. I stood there in my flowing black robe that felt more like a costume than a liturgical garment, and I hoped no one would notice that underneath that robe was nothing, not even hot air. In less than ten minutes I told them everything I knew about the mystery of the Christian faith, and still they expected more. I was thinking that they wanted me to explain the mystery of God, the Father, the Son, and the Holy Spirit, clarifying the doctrine of the Trinity followed by elucidation on concepts of sanctification, predestination, the total depravity of man, and substitutionary atonement. I dared not admit that I was still a little uncertain on some of these concepts.

Nevertheless, having donned my righteous rags, I stood behind the large oak pulpit and pontificated with variations on a theme for over eleven years. In truth, I was not the instructor, the teacher, or the preacher; the congregation was. Sunday after Sunday I would rise to the occasion, hoping that I could pull off this charade a while longer as I tried to make sense of denomination, doctrine, dogma, group dynamics, dysfunctional families, and the bride of Christ. In the course of time, the congregation instructed me in humility, acceptance, faith, despair, and hope.

The more I read what biblical scholars thought, what commentaries revealed, and what our forefathers (and a few—very few—foremothers) said about God and our place in this vast cosmos, the more I felt inadequate to be the leader of this shrinking congregation. How could I say to them something that would build their faith in God, cause them to rise as one to seek justice, or show them what it meant to walk humbly with God? I studied, asked questions of my pastor-friends, struggled with questions for which I could find no answer, and trusted God to be God because I found out that I certainly was not God. I was made in his image, Scripture told me, but Michelangelo's portrait of him made me doubt that. I did not look like God, but God did show me how to love and to create, and I think that is the way in which we are the most like him.

I have collected some ideas that have come to me through the years, and I keep spouting them like a leaky garden hose. For too long, I have been repeating my limited insights to the same dear people in my church. As the thoughts, questions, hopes, doubts, and epiphanies drip from that leaky garden hose, I think of a little water soaking into the soil and making a muddy, ruddy clay. Then I wonder if God still does things with clay, because if he does, I want to be available, pliable, and ready.

—Ragan Courtney

Prayer #999

Dear God,

If you are there,

How can you know me?

I am past middle-aged,

Filled with rage,

And emotionally catatonic.

I don't know which way to go,

So I curl up here—

Frightened,

Frozen,

Fetal.

I search my mind

As jumbled as an attic trunk of commonplace souvenirs.

I grope for an image to

Convey my desperate need.

Will this do?

God, I bleed

And breathe in

Oceans of cold, damp fear.

I drown in my own blood.

It mingles with earth, making ruddy, muddy clay.

Do you still do things with clay?

Could you do it right away?

Can salvation ever be instant gratification?

The World Is Spiritually Hungry

The world is spiritually hungry,

So we throw out stale religious crumbs

To tempt sparrow-souls

Into prim, proper, protestant prisons

Of ornate orthodoxy.

Trapped behind black iron bars of dogma and doctrine,

These fragile creatures are forced to consume

Inexact ideas of a deity

Who performs only after a litany of flattery.

Such an idea is

Pitifully diluted nourishment giving no nutritional sustenance.

Having consumed such a sour, scant meal,

Their spirits starve.

In desperate hunger they turn to any offered spirituality,

Drinking more and more thin milk

When they need bread and wine for life.

God, the bountiful provider, is outside their prison,

Bigger than their lamentable, clinical, systematic theologies.

The sparrow-souls seem too weak to soar

Across expansive vistas,

Through azure ethers

Hidden behind the thin purple pencil line of a horizon

Where freedom awaits.

Can God come to them once more?

The Way the Words Fall from My Mouth

The way the words fall from my mouth—

There is no rhyme or reason

That you can tell.

I don't really do this very well,

This wet vowel thing.

They are formed with rounded tones

Accompanied by clicks and clacks and fricative sounds

Trying to tell you something—

Now what was it?

Oh, yes,

I feel alone,

So I'm trying to tell you that

I am here.

These noises are not merely clicks and clacks and fricative sounds.

They are words

Telling you:

I read a story today,

Saw a nervous bird fly away,

Saw trees slowly sway

As the spirit moved them.

A daffodil bulb extended a small green hand up to me

From its clay pot.

The green pierced my eye.

Maybe that's the reason I wanted to cry,

Or is it because I have to try

So hard

To get you to hear what I have to say?

And who cares anyway?

I need to go where the wind leads me—

Or the spirit.

Maybe you can hear me then.

My vowels sound

More like the wind

In a whispery way

Trying to communicate—

What was it?

Oh, yes!

I'm here.

Idle Wish

I wish I could say what I actually feel.
I wish I could touch what is absolutely real.
I wish I could see how to be free.
I wish for one day—
Just for one day—
You could be me.

Of all the minds I've ever felt
Of all the tears I've ever wept
Of all the light I've ever seen
Of all the dreams I've ever dreamed
They are nothing without you.

Perhaps I know what I feel,
Perhaps I know what is real,
Perhaps I know how to be free,
Perhaps I know you can never be me.
But I wish you could,
I wish you could,
How I wish you could.

Weavings

The first threads were thinner,

More fragile

Than a spider's webs floating in sunlight.

They began to comingle like fibers in an invisible loom

As the warp and weft of our marriage began.

Who was the weaver of such gossamer-like strands?

The first encounter amazed.

Electricity was interwoven with finest strands of colorful silk

As the shuttle was hurled back and forth

With such grace and ease

That our initial response was to smile and blush.

I felt an awareness

More like a recognition of an ancient pattern.

It was the beginning of the tapestry

As two people were drawn to one another

And carefully woven together.

Somehow, I knew you,

Or, more nearly, recognized you

Standing there in the grand lobby,

Luggage at your side.

Palpitations and hormones

Caused my body to tremble and stir in a surprising way.

Dare I reveal my premature desire?

Is she the one who makes me inquire for answers

In an unspoken, unconscious code?

Like an infiltrator in a trench coat, I asked questions

That only another infiltrator could answer.
"Do you know First John, chapter four,
Verses seven through twenty-one?"
She gave a penetrating look. Inquisitive.
"It says, 'God is love.'"
"Yes, I know."
At yes, I had my answer.
She was the one for whom I had always searched
Always over there, not here. Not close by.
Over there.
Where I wanted to be.
I wanted to be next to her.
So we talked at length about the wonder of John's revelation as to the
identity
Of the Deity.

The threads began to thicken into yarn.
Warp and weft.
Shuttle moving back and forth
With regular rhythms.
There was red thread for passion,
White for a wedding,
Gold for wedding rings,
And a sprinkling of diamonds and emeralds
For extravagant surprises.
And the tapestry grew
With years and tears and joy,
Countless family and friends

Adding texture as the weaving became
Alive with laughter, music, poetry, and drama.
Nothing more alive than children
As the color of creation's source was
Carefully integrated into thick, soft yarns
That gave warmth to cribs and nurseries,
And sweaters and caps,
And scarves and socks,
And a family that cuddled
And loved.
All those textures and colors,
Wools, silks,
Silver threads and gold,
Dreams and desires,
Faith and failings,
Wounds and healings,
Commitments and love
Tied to a branch
Growing from the Vine
Waving in gratitude
For years.

The Calling

The call came early,

Softly so as not to frighten.

It was a spirit wooing him.

He did not know exactly who that spirit was.

But the call reassured him that it was permissible to feel different,

Feel alone,

Find refuge in the tall oak in the backyard,

Sit in the uppermost branches

And let the wind rock him as it danced with the tree.

He would let his mind soar, sometimes back to earlier days when he was

Flash Gordon,

Roy Rogers,

A Native American,

A Soldier.

There was no limit to the places or people available to him;

But even in the ethereal world of fantasy,

He was always aware of the call,

If not what it was a call *to* or *for*.

Then he would hear the sound of his name sung

By his mother calling him back to her reality.

Or was it the sound of the wind calling

Through the trees,

Or could it be the sound of the world tomorrow

Urging him forward?

It was not long before the source of the call came

Screaming into his mind like the sharp, splitting sound of a trumpet.

He was in church at the yearly revival

When the Holy Spirit arrived, programmed by committee to save souls.

The traveling evangelist preached,

Told heartbreaking stories of people who were

Planning on *making-a-public-profession-of-faith-in-*

Jesus-Christ-as-their-personal-Savior

When they were tragically killed only to have to spend

Eternity in hell

Where-the-worm-never-dies-and-the-flame-is-not-quenched!

Oh, the horror of it!

Poor little blonde girl dead,

Having to stand before God alone

A-damned-sinner.

Sweet Jesus,

Sweet, merciful Jesus was not—

Could not—be beside her to explain

That she could not come into heaven because she

Had no personal relationship with him,

She had *put it-off-once-too-often*

Not realizing that *the-Spirit-of-God-would-not-always-strive-with-her.*

So she fell

Like a lump of coal

Down,

Down,

Down

Into the bottomless,

Which—uh oh—did have a bottom after all,

A boiling, bubbling, bottom called hell.

And then the traveling evangelist told of all those who would

Spend eternity in a Godless hell because I—an eleven-year-old—

Did not witness to them and lead them *to-a-saving-knowledge-of-Jesus-*

Christ-as-their-personal-Savior,

And in that last day when we all stood before

The Almighty,

Omnipotent, omnipresent, omniscient Father/Judge—

As my friends were cast out and down,

I would see the accusing look in their eyes.

I would hear them cry out,

"Why didn't you tell me about Je-

eee-

eee-susss?"

In horror I would watch them as he damned these whom he loved enough

To send his Son to die for,

But not enough to excuse them from hell because

I didn't tell them the gospel story.

In order for me to stand on the right hand of the Father next to my

Best friend, Jesus,

I had to walk the church aisle, repent—again and again,

And have the congregation file by shaking my hand,

Thereby affirming that I was the best little boy in the entire church.

As they whispered religious encouragement into my innocent ear

Their breaths were like a hot, scorching wind,

And it was *that* call that I had to obey,

Or else . . .

Set in Stone

When concepts of God solidify,
Do they congeal
Like a blood clot?
Or do they concretize like a millstone
And drag us down to murky depths
Where decaying fishermen
Prostrate themselves across
Sunken treasure chests,
Where forgotten jewels lie in waiting
Eternally brilliant,
Longing to be retrieved,
To reflect the Light again?

I Read Poets and Prophets

I read poets and prophets,
Scholars and theologians,
Hoping to find insight,
Enlightenment, knowledge,
As their words whirl around
The surface of my mind
Like skaters on a frozen pond.
I am anxious because the ice is thin,
But how else except by following the swirls of the writer's doodlings
Shall I find the answer
To the questions that make me wonder?
Do I find the answers in the book
That opens with three haunting, taunting words:
"In the beginning?"

They do not satisfy
Because I immediately want to ask:
What was before the beginning?
What began?
Who or what began it?
And then the faint early light
Taps on my window before it
Gently slips into my house,
Revealing what else is:
Trees and leaves,
A man walking his dog,

A car pulling out from the intersection
At my corner.
My eyes drink in this daily scene yet again,
And I am comforted by ritual observation,
As my heart sighs
Opening to another day,
Loving the sight of the trees and leaves
And the people on their way.

Where are they going,
The trees and leaves and people?
Are they merely passing like actors across the stage,
Through the dark curtain
To the light?

Will I ever know why?
Perhaps I look too hard
And the answer is like the trees and leaves
In my own yard.

Again the book called Holy
With all those heavy, prophetic words
Glides over the thin, brittle
Covering of my mind
As I say out loud,
"In the beginning God . . . "

Is it simplistic or odd

That I take comfort in these ancient words?

As I drink my second cup of coffee,

The thin, brittle

Covering of my mind

Cracks under the weight of the word

God,

And the light melts the ice.

Sweet Vengeance

Lord, there is that child in me
That wants your blessing so all can see
What a special relationship I have with the deity.
Sometimes I am jealous that you
Could love others as you do,
And I hate to admit that it is true
You love us all individually,
Equally.
Like the Psalmist, I want to be closest to your heart.
And like the disciples, in your kingdom
I want a larger part.
I easily fathomed what David meant
In his Twenty-third Psalm when I read,
"In front of my enemies,
Give me a bigger spread!"
And Lord, you who are holy and sovereign,
And fill men's hearts with dread,
Would you see to it
That all my enemies are struck dead?
Oh, and yes, Lord, in agony
As they close their eyes to go,
Let them hear me whisper,
"I told you so!"

Louder

Sir?

What is it that you want?

Speak up, please,

I can barely hear you.

You hang around on the other side of the screen door

Out of sight and barely audible

In whispers more muffled than a moth's wings

Fluttering futilely against the overstretched rusted wire.

God, why are you concealed still?

Speak up, please.

I thought that the veil of the temple has been ripped from top

To bottom,

And you had issued forth like rushing water,

Scalding steam,

Torrents of tears

After Jesus had died

Making it possible for us to enter the Holy of Holies,

Become priests.

That doesn't seem to be available for me—

That priesthood thing—

So there must have been a slight misunderstanding.

Otherwise,

Why can't I hear you more distinctly?

If you can create radio waves,

And digital sound, and ears;

Would you figure out a way for me to hear you more clearly?

I have a sinking feeling that it is my fault,
This deafness.

Revive Us Again

Lord,
I know it is me who has
Faded and withered
And not from any fault of yours;
But I've made so many tours
And spoken so glibly the language of Zion
That I would be lying
If I did not admit
I would like to quit.
I feel as dried up and phony
As those silly Vacation Bible School flowers
Made of gilded macaroni.
It is you, Lord, which can bring blooms to the desert
And morning light to the sky.
It is you, Lord, who can quicken my spirit
And hear my dust-choked soul begin to cry,
Not only for revival,
But survival.

Hawkers and Mockers
(A visit to Jerusalem)

Hawkers and mockers,

Believers and deceivers,

Bric-a-brac and knickknacks,

Children selling olive branches for a dollar,

Pre-recorded calls to prayer for faithful Muslims

From multitudinous minarets,

The drone of Jewish men groaning prayers

At the Wailing Wall,

The bleating of the herds of wide-eyed

Christian pilgrims

Darting wherever their

Rent-a-Shepherd leads them.

The tumult of frantic traffic,

The continued digging of archaeologist—

Like scarab beetles burrowing in dung,

Like maggots in holy carrion—

Bombard us.

We bow to enter the Church of the Nativity

As a stout woman

With no sense of decorum or civility

Presses a group of Asian pilgrims

To the front of the line.

(The last shall be first?)

Other busy guides

Chant their endless litany:

"It is believed that . . . "

Or "Tradition has it that . . . "

To the mesmerized flock,

As the clock determines

What time is available before

The next group is due.

On every wall

And over the altar

Are faces of the Virgin and Child,

Variations on a theme.

The silent two seem to peer

Through the haze of

Candle soot,

Dust,

Incense,

And the damp breath of murmured prayers

Settling for eons

Like a veil on a bride.

Her eyes are unfocused

As she sits posed and poised,

Waiting for all the pandemonium to pass.

Is she remembering an earlier time,

When she held that

Tiny, newborn infant

To her virgin's breast,

Offering warmth,

Succor,

And as much protection from the world

As innocence and love can afford?
Oh, Divine Incarnation,
We worship you
In a temple far away from
Peddlers of postcards and religion.
We worship you in the Holy of Holies of our hearts
As we marvel the meaning of the name,
Emmanuel.

Pearl of Great Price

Sear over.

Seal up.

Lock and don't look

At that tiny festering part of your brain.

It is a wound healing.

An incision

Where a growth was removed,

Nipped

In full flower.

Sear over.

Seal up.

Cover layer upon layer,

Layer upon layer,

Layer upon layer

Of protective tissue.

Maybe tomorrow

When you look at it,

It won't be a scar,

But a pearl.

To a Young Theologian

Young theologian, fear not.
Fear not during your deep, dark
Night of despair.
I have been there,
And the night is black and deep,
And horrors seem to seep through the walls
Like a mist that rolls silently down the halls
Of your mind.
And no one seems to hear
Desperate, urgent calls
For light.
There await astounding sights
Filled with fright
Of what might devour you
And your well-designed, systematic theology.
The science of God must never be exact.
Exactness is too small a temple for God's house.
That Spirit can only be housed
In a tabernacle as big as truth.
As the deity is revealed
You will heal,
And each healing comes in a different way.
Mine came after the fight ended.
I had surrendered,
Finding myself befriended after my fall.

I fell into a well with no bottom;

Its walls, onyx.

Faith fled.

Love was nowhere to be seen.

Perhaps it was hidden

Behind an ornate, oriental screen.

Doubt and fear

Emerged like gladiators,

Powerful, armed, dim-witted, and drooling

Eager to devour every ounce

Of hope I had.

They feasted, gorged, glutted,

Sated themselves

Leaving me a stripped spent corpse.

In the twinkling of an eye—or three days—

Or a lifetime—I can't remember—

I awoke.

Tender Grace was stroking

My tearstained face

Holding my empty, broken heart.

I had to start all over to fill it.

This time I was determined

To fill it with truth and love—

No systematic theology.

I could do that later,

After I had put my fingers

Into his nail prints.

Young theologian,

Surrender to your doubt.
Your mind can accommodate
Conceptions of God,
Plus the universe.
Chaos and order.
Doubt and faith.
And all the heart can hold.

The Cross Is Protestant Bare

The cross is Protestant bare,

Stark,

Bleak,

Empty.

Hanging in the pristine American sanctuary

Of the University Presbyterian Church

Where iconoclasts seem to have won

A centuries-old war over

Sacred accoutrement.

I long to see a crucifix

Like the one in Sabanagrande, Honduras—

All tortured and grotesque,

Twisted in agony

And congruent with the understanding

Of passionate brown peasants who

For centuries have respectfully covered his nakedness

And used vibrant

Red, lead-based paint

Like cosmetics

To emphasize the finer points of the crucifixion:

Blood dripping from the thorns,

His hands,

His beautiful, wounded feet,

Flowing in little rivulets

And pouring in torrents from his side.

Their creativity cannot be denied

As I looked at his knees

Like theirs,

Bloody from one fall too many.

His chest no longer heaves

But seems to arch

As though attached to a marionette's string tugging upward,

Or a heart trying to take flight and pulling the body toward release.

The candles flicker.

The incense rises.

The peasants hunch forward,

Bent and broken before the only one more broken than they.

They understand brokenness and they pray

Kyrie, eleison.

Christe, eleison.

Kyrie, eleison.

The glass eyes set in the bowed head of the sacrificed Christ

Reflect the candle light from the church

Like small, convex mirrors.

And the light, a visible echo of whispered prayer,

Makes him seem near to them.

It was merely a craftsman whim—those glass eyes—

Poorly executed, really;

But this crucifix moves me to silence

And I stay and pray.

Cain's Markings

Woe is me for I am undone,

And the only distraction I am allowed is chewing my tongue.

Pain and salty blood, sacred elements for a dark communion,

As I long for union.

My deep self watches in amazement

As my incarnate self runs in disquiet directions,

Desperate with desire for completion.

There is the feeling of not belonging,

Of being detached.

The gate to the green Garden of Eden

Is latched,

And I hold on to its connecting fence post

As the pull of the void tugs my feet from under me

And I flap like a flag, a desperate signal of distress

Unfurled against a backdrop of blackest night.

I am Cain.

I live outside the garden

In a faraway country of Nod,

A solitary exile,

Banished

To a world of evolving pain.

Abandoned like no other—

I miss my brother!

I miss my brother!

Why is he so still?

What does this word mean? "Kill."

Is there no one
To help me feel complete
To bathe my bruised psyche,
To wash my bleeding, dirty feet?
Woe is me for I am undone.
Is there no one
Who can help bear the pain
Of the shame of Cain?

They Shall See God
(For Dr. Frank Tupper)

"Blessed are the pure in heart for they shall see God,"

Jesus said.

Is it too late,

Too late for me to be pure in heart?

Maybe I was—once.

Maybe,

When I was little and protected by my sweet, young mother

Who only exposed me to gentle things like

Lullabies, warm summer rains, soft arms,

Puppies, a baby sister so small that she could sleep on a pillow

Like a tiny fairy princess,

Poems, stories with happy-ever-after endings,

Cool afternoon naps with open windows and lacy, white curtains

Slowly, gracefully dancing

With the invisible, wandering wind

That had just arrived from a cooler climate.

Innocent, pure in heart,

Life before the age of accountability

When I sang,

"Jesus loves me

This I know . . ."

Life before I knew of the terrible theology of the total depravity of man.

At what unsuspecting moment did I cross over from

Purity to impure,

Innocence to guilty,

Blameless to accountable

When did the sweet phrase of Jesus loves me change to

You are a God damned sinner?

But it happened.

I am assured it happened

Because I know I am not pure in heart.

Still I long so to see

The one who is spirit and truth,

Who is creator of all,

Who holds the world in his hands carefully

Like a child holds a blue robin's egg,

Who is the first and final proof

That he is.

And it is proof that I need.

Proof stronger than my fragile faith

Has been able to provide.

I want to see past these people

And those people,

The sick and the dying,

The infected ones,

The homeless ones,

The war-weary refugees,

The dark innocents with fly-encrusted eyes

Who have not crossed the mysterious boundary

That separates those loved by Jesus

From those damned by God.

Is it too late for me?

Can I ever see,

Rising in all his majesty
From this roiling, writhing sea of humanity,
The Son of Man,
Who reveals the Supreme Deity
Who made me like him,
Pure in heart?

Them and Us

They are not like us.
They are over there
With funny eyes and strangely colored skin,
And they are most definitely not like us!
Their ideas differ from ours.
Their clothes differ.
Their hair differs.
Their smells differ.
Their god differs.
So we will surreptitiously ridicule them—
For fear we appear judgmental and
Accidentally reveal our suppressed superiority to them,
Because we are made in the image of *that* I Am.
They, mere copies of copies of irregular copies.
They pray that way,
Worship that way,
Sing that way,
And it is painfully obvious that
Their way is not our way,
And our way is the way of true enlightenment
And ultimate orthodoxy.
They try, poor things, but they fail to be like us.
It is clear.
They were predestined for inferiority,
Eternal damnation.
Soaring is not feasible for clods.

They were not meant ultimately to commune with God.

They are not like us.

Lines of People
(For Ken Medema)

Lines of people scraping empty bowls,
Huddled masses in the winter wearing
Hand-me-down, patched holes.
Soldiers marching back and forth across the land,
Preachers screaming about the son of man who said:
"Come, let us reason together."
"Come," blare politicians in handsome, gray suits;
"Come," shriek preachers in patent leather boots;
"Where?" whisper people sitting on a pew;
"Where?" ask the children stretching for a better view
Of the screaming leaders calling:
"Come.

Come.

Come."
As they beat the air like an empty, hollow drum.
"Hallelujah!" they all shout to fill in the blanks.
"Hallelujah!" they all shout at the swelling of their ranks.
"Hallelujah to the Son of Man.
Lead, guide, and direct us to the Promised Land.
Keep us always in thy sight.
Let us know that we are right,
And stronger,
And blest
Better than all the rest,
Who are publicans and sinners,

Disgusting bartenders,
Drunkards and harlots.
(Thank God, *our* sins were never scarlet, only shocking pink.)
We are still the majority
In this land of the free."

Lines of people scraping empty bowls.
Huddled masses in the winter wearing
Hand-me-down, patched holes.
Teachers talking to empty, wooden chairs.
Black-light Jesus posters being sold at crowded state fairs.
All buy the posters,
But no one cares
That their iridescent icon
Represents the one who said:
"Come, let us reason together."

White Flags

Not all wars are obvious.

Lord, my bellicosity occurs on interior battlefields.

I think it has to do with pride

Because I know what is required of me—

Surrender.

I have been a rebellion unto myself.

I second-guess what I know is right.

I start every day with a ripe rationalization.

I deny this,

Reinterpret that.

I lie to myself saying that I deserve this or that favor.

I run up my own banner,

And proclaim

That I am my own man—

King of my own domain.

But—if the truth be known—

I am not doing so well with governing myself.

It feels more like a war.

Could you come to my defense?

See past my bold pretense

To my need to stop this clash.

I have been brash.

Would you look past this military pomp

And see this little white flag waving

Surrender?

Inner Wars

Echoing down the battle-worn streets of my memory
Are the cruel booted marches
Of Man's armies
Crushing tender grasses
Ripping open the passive Earth
And tearing out the innards
Through planetary wounds.
And the cruel booted marches
Of Man's armies
Fighting for fatherland,
And honor,
And God,
And orthodoxy.
Stomp!
Stomp!
Stomp in step
On the bleeding clay of God's tender creation.
Yet, in my heart, I also hear
The solitary footfalls
Of bare feet on Galilean roads
Gently reminding me of peace.
Not the world's peace,
Rather, His peace.
His words tug at my soul
More steadily than the tide pulls at the sea.
When he says:

Love God,
Your neighbor,
Your enemy.
I hear the truth,
And I long to shuck my shoes
And walk barefoot with him.
I don't.
Instead, I listen to liars and politicians tell me
I must take care of Number One.
I must fight for what's mine
Or theirs, if my country wants it.
Fight!
Fight!
Fight the fight
Or be prepared to.
That is the reality of the world today.
So what do I say?
Here, take my money,
Take my sons and daughters
And offer them like Isaacs
On the altar of Nationalism.
Take all resources to build defenses,
Atomic fences.
Keep peace by preparing for war.
Rule by might, power, and fear.
But in my inner ear I hear
Solitary footsteps of bare feet
Walking on . . .
Alone.

Our Vantage Point

It is clean,

Antiseptic.

Sharp lines on scopes

Focus our sights on alien targets.

Then little puffs of smoke signal us

That we have scored another point,

And we are sure to win this video game—

A top seller to the youth of our country

Marketed as "WAR!"

Available at a mall near you.

Our electronic entertainment

Is a source of great pride.

It keeps us detached and diverted

As we train our children

In the skills of blowing up people and things.

We never hear the screams of distant sufferers,

Traumatized children, babies wounded in their dying mother's arms.

Never see that the feet that flee in terror

Over blackened ruins

Leave footprints of ash

Across our industrialized souls.

O God, is this what you mean

When you say we should love our enemies?

Or does that entreaty only apply

In times of peace?

God, I have not had time to grieve

The last carnage so complete that thousands upon thousands no longer
live.
Too soon war returns.
I need time to weep
For all unholy alliances, compromises, and maybes,
For war, destruction, and innocent, dead babies.

Apocalypse

There are dreams and visions and prophets,
And faded, old photographs;
Roller coasters, screams, and politicians,
And painted clowns with pre-recorded, mechanical laughs.
There are wheat fields, cornfields, and mine fields,
And fields of Flanders covered with blood.
And widows weeping for their dead—
Searching through empty promises buried in all that red mud
To a war that will not, cannot heal
A world gashed, bleeding, and ignored
Like a bag lady mugged for the greasy bills
Hidden in her tattered clothes, drenched with gore.
Her attacker calls laughingly from the shadow,
Tossing her pitiful treasure to the night,
"Thank you so much for the thrill, my dear.
I would stay, but it's late,
And you are a frightful sight."

Seeing her gurgling mouth mime
A silent plea to the air,
Frozen, the crowd watches the agony of the old woman
As though struck in Madame Tussauds' wax poses
In someone's insane nightmare.
No one moves to help the victim from the street.
Instead, as though on cue,
They step gingerly away on tiptoe

To keep her life's blood
From soiling the supple leather that covers each dancing shoe.

And the blood flows down the gutter,
And empties down the drain,
And the heavens weep acid tears
Mingled in the rain.
And laughter fills the streets,
And shadows fill their hearts.
And the liar keeps on lying,
And the world seems dark.
The one who loved her first,
And fathered each son and daughter,
Who wrapped her tenderly in morning mist,
And bathed her with holy water,
Walked her rocky beaches,
And sailed her stormy seas,
Marveled at her sunsets,
And died upon her trees,
Looked at her lying there
Used and broken and old,
Knelt beside her in the filth
Remembering clearly what prophets foretold.
He took his sleeve with compassion,
And wiped her bleeding brow,
"I understand your suffering, Beloved.
I love you then:
I love you now."

And he sighed so softly
Those close by did not hear
Comfort as tender as rustled wings
Falling on her ear.
And a tambourine started playing
And a street preacher screamed to all,
"Repent! The end is near, you vipers.
Hear me before it's too late.
There is no curtain call."

The crowd began to smile,
Then they began to murmur,
But the dying woman and her friend
Heard something that sounded like righteous thunder.
And the preacher screamed louder,
And the people mocked in mirth,
But the friend whispered to her,
"I see a new heaven,
And a new earth."

And the blood flowed down the river
And emptied down the drain,
And the heavens wept acid tears
Mingled in the rain.
As the blood continues flowing,
Heaven greets with cheers
The woman without spot or blemish
Smiling as he dries her tears.

Waiting

Waiting.

Life is spent waiting

Swimming in an ocean of ideas

Buffeted by thoughts of God

While all the culture idols raise their ugly heads

And reveal all their whores

On sullied beds

Where nothing good was conceived

Just greed

With the conjoined need to have more and more

Even if it makes Christ bleed.

When the time for waiting has past,

Leaving you to see clearer at last,

What is revealed?

From this place there is the sight of love shyly concealed,

Too many times of not professing

The deep spiritual tie that binds

Man to wife to child,

To a greater family;

Not confessing, "I love you," enough

And letting them all be

Who they are.

Is that a star?

No, it is light in a tunnel

Where decades of episodes are funneled

Through an opening

Smaller than a pinprick

Only to erupt into

A magnificent realm of light

Where there is

More life,

Luminescence,

Love,

And understanding that God no longer buffets,

Rather, embraces.

Hope Is Everywhere

Hope is everywhere
Like air,
But we don't see it.
The citizens around Bethlehem
Must not have looked up that night.
Maybe their hope was dim or gone.
But that night;
Four million
Four hundred
And forty-four thousand
Angels singing
(And that's a lot of angels)
Paraded through a split in time.
The swoosh of their wings swept
Clouds away,
Webs away,
Fear away.
They laughed
And sang
Four million four hundred
And forty-four thousand
New songs about
The Holy One,
God's baby Son.
"And the shepherds were sore afraid
And the angel said unto them:
'Fear not; for BEHOLD!'"

Angels Dancing

Like pinpricks in a black shade
The stars flicker intensely over the winter hills,
Letting little glimmers of light escape.
As the shepherds
Talk softly in the cold night,
Angels appear and begin to dance
On points of light
Sharper than needles,
Prickly like straw on a newborn baby's skin,
Thorny foreshadowing of incarnation.
And the shepherds fall down in terror
At all the dancing angels
Whirling, fluttering in robes
Like colorful aurora borealis.
"Fear not!
For we bring you good tidings of great joy.
For unto you is born a Savior!"
They sing in the language of angels.
The huddled shepherds marvel at the music
And the entire heavenly host
Dancing on the heads of pins.
How many?
As many as needs be to proclaim:
The tabernacle of God
Is with mankind,
And he will dwell with them.

They shall be his people,
And he will be their God!

The Old, Wise Ones

Do we listen to them,

The old, wise ones

Who have heard the whispered voice of God?

Do we deny their vision,

Dismiss as superstition

Warnings

Of destruction

As the pillars of the temple are eroded

By reptilian tongues licking Lot's wife's feet?

Whole sections of society are collapsing

Beneath the briny depths of the Dead Sea's heavy waters

As angels flutter about,

Mouths opened wide in silent screams.

Plucked, blood-tipped feathers fall like confetti

Scattered in a hellish dream;

Decisions are fraught with painful consequences,

As Christ's name is battered about like a badminton birdie

In a storm of religious pretension.

And sages, Pharisees, and sibyls

Conjecture, divine, and foretell,

Breathing apocalyptic warnings

Of battles, children's blood,

And an up-to-date meaning of hell.

So how do you speak to us,

The obstinate ones?

Prophets, ancient scriptures,

Two-bit plastic preachers
Hawking cheap grace on their TV show?
Or as trusted friend's call filled with foreboding?
How can we discern
The infinite lessons you have for us to learn,
If we ignore
The old, wise ones
Who have heard the whispered voice of God
Repeating those breathtaking words
That are hurled across the cosmos
To their hearts.
Their dry, raspy voices utter such
Profundities that Mt. Sinai shakes
In sympathetic response,
Remembering the time Jehovah walked
On its craggy
Pinnacle.
But we hear only political pundits
And the clarion call of Mammon.
I fear
We do not hear
The old, wise ones.

Heart Song

The sound is low—
Beneath the rumble of the residual roar
Of the first vital moment
Eons ago.
It is beneath silence
And can only be heard when
An ear is pressed to God's chest
As one kneels in adoration.
The rhythm comforts
Like a mother's heart-song to her unborn,
Filling up all available void with
Regular rhythms of being.
That sound is
The basis of our reality—
I Am . . . I Am . . . I Am,
A remembered rhythmic lullaby for the sin-sick soul
Consumed with the longing of an
Ongoing homecoming.

I Sit Still

I sit still in the brown-flecked midst
Of all those nervous sparrows
Pecking at stale bread
Dropped on the side of the street
By some wandering beggar.
They peck and pull,
Attack and tear,
Sustaining life from a carelessly tossed crust,
And I sustain life by observing them.
Should a vehicle rumble too near, they flutter away,
And chirp tales of derring-do,
And the crumbs they almost had.
Twittering around my rusty, crusty, peeling park bench,
They wrench my fainting heart with their nervous tenacity.

Annunciation

A startling appearance of a shining angel ephemeral as a ghost

Was cause for fear.

Either she had lost her mind at an early age,

Or God had some terrible news for her.

It was the latter.

"Don't be afraid," the angel said

To the young girl who was about her own business.

Why did the angel think that she would be afraid?

A noise like a trumpet, or all trumpets—

A smell like a rose, or all roses—

Huge colorful wings, unfolding

Like dual sunrises—

East and west simultaneously,

Shekinah glory from God's throne lighting up her humble home,

A word terrifying to her virgin ears.

"You shall have a Son, and his name will be Jesus."

"But I am not married. I have never . . . "

"The Holy Spirit shall overshadow you."

"Yes, but how?"

"With God all things are possible."

"Yes, but . . . "

"Your son will reign over the House of Jacob forever, and of his kingdom,

there

Shall be no end."

"Yes, but . . . "

"Be not afraid."

"Yes, but . . .
I am."

Keeping X in Xmas

A list,

Endless

Family and friends,

Obligations

All a blur,

Presents for sake of presents.

Rushing joylessly from car to store

From mall to mall,

Crying out in frustration

That no one hears.

The belfries filled with the echoes of happier sounds

Swing the bronze bells back and forth leisurely

For no apparent purpose

Since the season has nothing to do anymore with its original intent.

What to give the one whose birth we celebrate?

A treasure in an earthen vessel would be appropriate,

But this vessel has been shattered

And all of the contents lost

So there is no thing

Nothing,

Nada,

Zip

To offer the celebrant—

Except brokenness,

Pieces,

Dried-up dreams

Like brittle residue,
Self-pity.
Dare I offer him heartache,
A life gone wrong,
Misery,
A strident, melancholy song
As hollow as the reverberations
In the ancient bells
With their reminder of earlier celebrations?

Betrayer
(*Jesus talks to Judas*)

I called you friend,

Even though I saw your uncertainty.

Your dark eyes used to look right into mine, penetrating—

Always searching.

But the day came when you averted those eyes,

Looking at your feet or some distant, imaginary bird circling

Just above my shoulder

When you spoke to me.

I heard the pouch of coins jingle as you absentmindedly played with it

Like worry beads.

Why were you worried?

Did you think that kingdom dreams would not sustain us?

Since the Kingdom of God seemed too ethereal for you,

I entrusted you with tangible things that made your heart flutter.

I let you carry the paltry coins,

But they did not satisfy you.

They never do.

Then I gave you a seat of honor at the Passover meal—

My last supper with you,

But it was a gesture not grasped.

Even sopping up gravy with my own bread and offering it to you

A sign of deep affection and intimacy

You failed to comprehend.

Later, when you kissed me in the garden of Gethsemane,

Your lips were already cold as death

And your dark eyes still do not look at me.

Could they not see me?

Or did they dare not see me?

Had you walked along with me for all this time and not heard me?

Your kiss was not the final act of betrayal—

And I know betrayal well—

It was the rope.

Had you waited,

You would have seen me hanging between two thieves,

And you would have known I forgive thieves.

Then you could have told how the Kingdom of God

Does not have silver or gold as its currency,

Rather love,

Which is so readily exchanged for forgiveness.

Poor Judas,

You did not know what you were doing.

Corpus Christi
(Christ's POV)

I see them circling,

Circling,

Circling

Specks in the distance coming out of the gathering clouds.

Is it Michael coming to comfort me with his legions of angels?

No.

I can see wings through the blood and tears in my eyes.

Is it the bountiful Spirit in the form of doves coming to affirm my

obedience?

No.

The wings are silent and powerful.

They unfurl like a black scroll,

And I recognize them.

Creatures drawn to death

Like a baby to his mother's breast.

O, God, has it come to this?

Vultures above me

Slowly circling toward my dying flesh

And vulturous crowds

Circling, cursing, jeering,

Their gnarled fingers like talons

Longing to rend my flesh.

They don't know what they are doing.

Father, forgive them.

Where are my friends?

Have I been deserted

Except for these buzzing flies?

God, have you left me here with all these flies and their lord?

Oh, I see friends over there huddled together.

It breaks my heart to see them weeping.

John standing by Mother,

Such a friend.

Oh, Mother, do you know how much I love you, really love you?

Thank you for what you have done.

John—John, take care of her.

She is so fragile, so tender, so—Mother.

I'm thirsty.

My head aches.

These thorns like hornets are unrelenting.

My lungs feel as though they are on fire.

Please. Please. Please.

How much longer does this have to go on?

Hunger and Thirst

Christ,

I cannot get enough of you.

I want to take you into me—

My heart,

My mind,

My soul—

But you flicker elusively around me.

I stand like a silent, white, wax candle.

You?—The flame.

You burn me,

You consume me,

You reduce me to waxen tears.

Christ,

I am mad with hunger

To consume your body,

Drink your blood.

Intoxicated with the idea of you,

I want to wrap myself in the paraments;

And like a pagan reborn, dance and dance in the shadowy nave of your

church

To rhythms in my heart pounding out ceaseless praise

Like hymns, like love songs of holy longing.

Color streaming through the stained glass metamorphoses me

From a mere mortal to a great, variegated golden koi.

I submerge myself in the cool reservoir of the baptismal fount,

Once more an innocent baby boy

Breathing in deep draughts of holy water.
I am
Bathed in bliss only to burst forth
Newer than Lazarus.
Christ,
I cannot get enough of you!

Burning Mystery

Burning mystery,

Shimmering sands,

Shuffling feet of great desert beasts,

Blinding sun sentenced to burn for eternity,

Hanging like a torch,

Consuming the cloudless ethers,

A refiner's fire.

Thorns,

Lizards,

Skeletal remains of ancient creatures,

Baked earth, acrid pools,

Dry palms with brittle leaves,

Thirsty pilgrims,

Sucking stones in agonizing thirst,

Licking mud

For the dark remnants

Of earlier wet blessings.

We are frightened,

Aimless wayfarers.

Oh, ancient God of nomads

With invisible feet,

We have lost our way.

The Pillar of Fire does not lead us,

Only scorches.

The Pillar of Smoke

Does not direct us,

Only obscures.

Where are you?

Are you over the flaming horizon

Beside a tranquil pool

In a verdant garden

Waiting,

Or is that a pitiful mirage?

Has the way been made ready?

Has the fierce guardian angel

With the steadfast sword

Relaxed his vigilant duty enough to let

Us back into your presence

Where grace bathes our parched souls?

Oh, fierce desert God of Abraham, Isaac, and Jacob,

Will you be our oasis,

Or is it all a mirage

Fading like hope?

Thoughts on Seeing for the First Time

To have never seen light,
But to have felt the sun's glow and understand
That warmth was caused by light,
Makes me yearn to see this thing that feels so gentle on the cheek.
Yellow. My mother called the sun—yellow.
Is she—being so warm and gentle—yellow, also?

To have never seen a star,
But to hear my mother try to describe a small speck of light in the
evening sky
Like a tiny pebble shiny on the seashore
Makes me yearn to grasp a handful of stars and pour them into her lap.

And green!
What is green?
To feel the grass tickle bare feet,
To pluck an olive branch
And be told that it is green, as I smell crushed leaves,
Makes me wonder if everything is green, and does green always tickle?

Then blue—
What does the huge sky look like all blue?
And the lake and water
That cools my tongue quenching my thirst,
All blue?
Do I become blue when she pours water over me?
I would love to see blue.

And red.
Like hot coals glowing.
Mother said that berries are red.
Do they glow on bushes,
Burning with life and energy
Like the bush Moses saw?
Is red sour or sweet?

And how can I comprehend a rainbow?
Colors like ribbons arching across the sky.
I would so love to see a rainbow.
If I could fly, I would soar up there with the birds
And wrap myself in all those colors,
And say hello to God.
Could I see a bird's song?
That must be a lovely color.

And then one day after a lifetime of wondering,
A man came to me and smeared my eyelids with clay, brown.
"Go bathe at the Pool of Siloam," he said.
I did.
Black dissolved
Into pink,
And I saw a confusing profusion of color,
More colors than I had names for.
I stood there speechless, drinking in all that light.
They called him a sinner.
I knew what that was,

And he was no sinner.
He was a prophet, at least,
Or the Messiah,
Because no one had ever opened the eyes of a man blind from birth.
And he did open my eyes,
And I looked into his eyes.
"That must be the color of eternity," I thought
As I knelt before him.

St. Genesius of Rome (died c. 286 or c. 303) is a legendary Christian saint and actor who acted in plays that mocked Christianity. It is said that one day while performing in a play that ridiculed Christianity, he had a conversion experience. He told what had happened to him and refused to deny his new faith even though ordered to do so by the emperor Diocletian. He was beheaded and became the patron saint of actors.

The Passion of St. Genesius

Around his neck he wore a medallion

On a silver chain

Of a saint who never was,

Some say.

St. Genesius,

Patron saint of the theater.

It hung there a sterling reminder

That theater is spiritual, fanciful, and hypocritical.

Nothing was what it seemed,

Certainly not the actor.

Wanting desperately to be adored,

He would drape a persona—

Any old persona—

Around his shoulders

Like a flowing, meretricious cape

As he whirled into the magnetic light,

Drawn to it like affection draws abused children.

He was often called on to perform during the Christmas season

Where he played various holy holiday roles:

Matthew, Mark, Peter, Simeon, Thomas

All telling their versions of the incarnation,

Annunciation,

Passion,

Resurrection,

Ascension.

The actor affected an unctuous, stained-glass voice,

Feigning piety

During performances.

For years people gathered to see the story reenacted.

Like thirsty children they drank in

The lights, costumes, music, and magic,

Their faces wet with wonder and shining in reflected theater lights.

The evenings were feasts of angel-food cake.

They did not know that the Greek word for actor

Was also the word for hypocrite,

But the actor knew.

Yes, he knew!

Then there came the time when the actor was on call

For yet another rehearsal where

Cues were given, lights were set, and blocking was finalized

For another telling of the story, a variation on the theme.

The room was filled with the sound

Of a well-run machine.

Another actor playing the crucified Christ

Casually lolled on the cross,

Waiting for the designer to set a lighting cue,

When suddenly, the Word became flesh,
Surprising the lead actor—the medal wearer.
Like Jacob wrestling the angel
The actor turned to the sham crucifix,
Becoming a silent, seething supplicant,
And pled for relief.
"You have it pretty easy, really," he thought.
"You hang up there for a few hours
While I've been on my cross for decades!
You always have God in your back pocket.
When he was not sending you flocks of angels to sing you lullabies,
He was deafening everyone with his booming voice
Thundering out across the river bank,
Affirming you and stating for all to hear
That you are his beloved son in whom he is well pleased!
Now I know a Roman cross was cruel,
But in a few hours you were home free.
And the entire time you were here, you never felt ashamed to be you!
You never had to apologize for anything.
Your parents were saints!
Here I am on this empty, lonely stage in deep pain
Racked with shame.
Who is to blame if I can't find God?
I feel terror in the thought of his absence.
I know hell well.
Incarnation, indeed!
You do not know what it means to be fully fallen,
To share in the lowest common denominator here,
Total depravity!"

The actor, dropping pretense
Started to weep.
And God began to speak,
Not in a voice like thunder,
But as softly as the dust mote that floated
Down from the cat-walk where the stagehands,
As remote as distant angels,
Focused lights.

God spoke:
"Spirit became flesh.
Put on skin.
Walked in your shoes.
Understands sin.
Does not condemn you.
Knows you personally, intimately.
He knows what you did, and why.
Do not cry,
Except for joy.
You are accepted, forgiven, and loved
Unconditionally by me.
Dear broken child, I know your misery
Because he walked where you walked,
And understands the mortal condition.
How I long for you to put on immortality,
To be completely who you were created to be.
This is the crux of the matter:
When he shouldered the burden,

He buckled under the weight of it
Like a wildflower crushed by itinerant flocks.
Now that burden is as light
As hoped-filled balloons tugging upward,
And ablaze with glory.
Examine the story you tell.
Transmit the truth of it
Like Mary Magdalene did with such sweet, female strength,
Such evangelistic fervor,
Such ecstatic joy
When she cried out, 'I have seen the Lord!'
Tell it like Paul when he said in Damascus,
'He is the Son of God.'
Tell it like Peter at Pentecost when he said,
'This Lord whom you crucified, God has made him both Lord and
Messiah.'
Tell it like Dietrich did in prison when he said,
'God's love lasts forever.'
Now I will tell you the highest truth,
The truth on which I have rested the foundations of all creation,
Beyond words, names, definitions,
Logic, doctrine, dogma, and mystery.
The truth is:
I love you because I Am and You Are mine."

And the actor portraying a saint
Became one because
He had opened his eyes.

He had seen the Word become flesh.
In helping to tell the story
He had acted his way to truth.
And when his belief failed,
He trusted God's love.

La Posada

Little homeless family huddled in an old car,
The night air is not filled with angelic voices,
Rather politicians yelling about family values,
Boundaries and walls
Until they are hoarse.
And you, little holy family,
Shiver
As your breath forms frost in the car windows.
The dash is not littered with
Gold, frankincense, or myrrh,
Rather empty fast-food boxes.
And there wrapped in an old blanket
Nestled close to his mother's heart
The least of these sleeps,
Waiting
For wise men to read the prophecy
And see what they should do about
This immigrant,
This refugee,
This newborn promise,
This holy child of God's.

It's the Simple Things that Get You

It's the simple things that get you.

For example:

Light.

It comes in waves from the distant realm of stars and suns.

It cascades, a dazzling delight,

Into azure pools of electric liquid

Bathing commonplace things,

Transfiguring meager flotsam and jetsam

Into treasures for a high-born king,

Revealing wonder waiting in the dark

Like a seed in the soil.

Surely this luminous substance is the discarded robe of

Zeus

Who now sleeps on the other side of Mt. Olympus

Having reconciled himself with Prometheus,

Or is it the afterglow of the Lord God's ecstasy

After pronouncing, "That is good!"

As he beheld his first day of creation?

Or is it the collective reflection

From the joy of all reality

At simply being?

Such an essential thing.

Simple, some say,

Such a brilliant thing.

Light!

The Wall

Not much is left of the Berlin wall

Physically,

Only cold, ghostly remains.

Its latest incarnation emerging on the Mexican/U.S.A. border,

In Israel separating:

Haves, have-nots

Us, Them

Belief, different belief

My God, your God

Ideas, dead dreams,

Thoughts that

Separate or unite

Imprison or liberate,

And contrary to Robert Frost's wit

Neither walls nor fences make good neighbors.

They isolate.

In time

The stone walls,

The brick walls,

The cement block walls

Crumble.

But those cold, shadowy walls are built with fear—

Invisible brick

By invisible brick—

To stand for all eternity.

Our inner worlds

Are stirred by a holy longing
Groping through the maze of our mind to find
The still center where heart,
Mind, and soul
Have no boundaries.
There that holy longing begins the
Herculean task of wall removal
As each stone,
Block,
Brick
Is lifted
One by one.
Through the first chink in the wall
Light floods in
Accompanied by the Light Bearer saying:
"Fear not. God is kinder than you imagined.
The world is simpler.
Love is available.
Let light melt those shadowy walls.
From the rubble build bridges.

Heroic Feelings

There are heroic feelings
Surrounding cataclysmic events such as
Rabid religious wars, famines, and threats of nuclear annihilation
That cause fearful emotions to seethe within our breast;
But we cannot express those
Sequestered, shrouded feelings
That taste like sour suspicions.
All we can phrase are fears, a fragile faith, and unfamiliarity,
So we groan inarticulate rumblings about the mystery
That only God can decipher.
God, our yearning for immortality—
Is it only our longing to return to you, our source?

Can we wholly attain that desire
When the sun novas,
And archives full of history,
Museums full of art,
Libraries full of books of foolishness and knowledge
Incinerate,
Along with our disremembered corner of an
Interminable universe?
When kit and kin and accomplishments
Combust into light,
A planetary conflagration,
That is a mere spark in the cosmos,
Light.

The stuff of which stars are made
Dark to light to dark,
Fear to faith to love,
Death to life to God?
When eternity opens up with
"Yes."

Voyage

I want to explore
The vast uncharted courses
Of my mind,
And unfalteringly
Report the discoveries.
With no navigating instruments,
No safari accoutrement,
No base camp to which I return.
I want to step out,
And step out,
And step out,
Until I journey from me
Into eternity.

The Story of the Antediluvian World

Before

Only darkness.

Soundless, motionless, eternally passive

Stretching backward and forward into fathomless emptiness,

Peaceful silence,

Absolute nothingness.

When somehow into this void there was an idea ejaculated,

Erupting into the darkness, arching across the empty black womb of night

Like a rainbow of light.

The flowing stream of ideas swelled into a torrent

Expanding.

Cascading into confusion.

The seed of all ideas that would ever be thought,

All color,

All sound,

All life,

All matter,

All spirit

Pulsating,

Swirling in unfathomed random motion,

Concentric circles colliding in glorious unrestraint,

Extravagant excess.

Like leviathan on the shore of time,

Chaos writhed, undulated in the sea of confusion,

Drank darkness like mother's milk,

Reveled in the newness of all that now is.

And there was a low, solid vibration like a cosmic heartbeat.
And in a great gasp, all that was filled the lungs of
The-One-Who-Thought,
And that one thought with a great shout,
"LIGHT!"
And there was light.
And it shimmered.
The small flickers of new ideas
Seemed to beckon across vast expanses of holy black like a beacon
Radiating from that shout.
The-One-Who-Thought danced for eons among the stars
Of shimmering colors that illuminated, revealing beauty in the chaos.
Some of the stars and suns clung to the thinker's robe like burrs to wool,
And dragged them across light years, dropping them here and there
As beauty dictated.
And light warmed, thawed, coaxed, and penetrated
Comets, planets, moons, cosmic dust.
Light invoked sighing, opening,
Changing its energy for another form of vitality.
The-One-Who-Thought laughed and thought some more,
Watching light embrace that which was created and
Eliciting more creation.
Earth was spun into being like a child's top
Dangling from gossamer gravity.
In the distance there lumbered across the grassy, curved plain
Beasts, small at first in the distance, and too numerous to count.
Great, gray-green, leaf-devouring, docile, creatures
Who existed merely to delight the thinker.

This one bartered one form of energy for another,

Seas and fishes

Forests and birds,

And scampering furry creatures.

And they multiplied,

And The-One-Who-Thought smiled, and patted, and caressed;

But the creatures did not smile back.

So another being was created to be like the creator,

Man in his own image—

Male and female created he them

And they thrilled him.

He gave them the run of the garden

Lush with life:

Green, dripping ferns,

Cool ponds and lakes,

Crashing seashores,

And creatures to tend.

They called He-Who-Thought—

God.

And way to the opposite end of the world God saved for himself

Cold, empty, barren ice fields;

Glittering flecks of stardust;

White expanses of accumulated layers of ice jewels

Holding most of the Earth's pristine water

Reminding him of the time he was alone.

Shame

It stood in the middle of the garden,

Towering, tantalizing.

Fruit—ripe and odoriferous—hung tentatively from its fabulous

branches.

Only a tiny graceful stem keeping that tasty morsel

From that dainty pink tongue

That was the first to drink from the Euphrates' pristine, virgin waters,

To taste the warm lips of the red-clay man,

To lick sweet nectar from a honeysuckle's cup,

To taste the tartness when she savored an orange.

But surely this fruit, so forbidden

And so delectable,

Could not be truly deadly.

Something in her told her that it was permissible

For her to taste.

Things were made

Expressly for her.

After all, she deserved even the forbidden

Because she was made in his image,

And she was the queen of the garden.

Why did brilliant parrots not

Shower her with their scarlet feathers,

Peacocks scatter their rich plumage—

Amethyst and iridescent greens—like an exotic carpet before her?

Did flowers with intoxicating fragrances not crown her noble head?

And to further convince her

That she deserved the fabulous fruit that was denied her,

Other came along.

"Eat," he urged.

"I have tasted it and it is divine. And so would you be—if you ate it."

"You tasted it?"

"Yesss."

"And it did not kill you?" she marveled.

"Look at me. Do I look dead? Am I not alive and talking to you?

Do you see how beautiful I am, lovely lady?—Eat."

Her delicate fingers encircled the succulent orb.

Her mouth wet with anticipation, bit—

Bit deep and ripped out soft, sweet flesh.

And it was good—

That was all.

No thunder, no lightning, no disapproving resounding voice.

And the sweet, swallowed shame

Tasted pleasurable.

Then it was that the wind began to blow—

Cool.

Cooler than ever before.

She began to shiver and long for Adam,

For she was afraid and cold

As the newness grew old.

After

In the years that followed

She would lie in Adam's arms trying to feel warmth again.

The canopy over their resting place

Became cruel briars, like a prison

Of iron lace.

And the sharp thorns like the claws of the animals

Always waiting to rend them.
She worried about the boys who slept nearby,
Pink, naked cubs snuggling for warmth
Under the skins of dead animals—
The very creatures with which she had
Run in open savannas.
Now their creature blood had turned the soil rusty red
As they—for a while—simply submitted in innocence—
Unsuspecting sacrifice—
To the new merciless stone knife.
They killed that they might cover with ill-gotten fur the hairless
nakedness
Of those creatures just a little lower than the angels.
Then she fed her family with what was left
Of those pitiful, bleeding carcasses.
As her incisors ripped into the succulent flesh,
Blood ran down her neck and dripped
Off her breast.
Her boys suckled there—
Blood and mother's milk.
Her confused mind called out to God,
Who used to come in the cool of the evening,
"What is happening to us?
Where are you?
Help us. Help us, please!"
As their jaws masticated
Flesh into pliable chunks,
They did not notice the serpent

As he slithered around the ground sounding like the soft rustle
Of dead leaves scattered by a fitful wind,
Trailing behind scurrying feet of frightened animals
Running from their human predator.
The scurrying became a stampede,
The stampede a riot,
The riot a revolt as the terrified animals
Fled from their fallen fellow creatures.
The pitiful animals would turn and attack the hunters,
Or flee from the agonizing death
They feared at the hands of their former masters.
Dust whirled around the woman.
Screaming pierced her ears and her heart.
Chaos was rampant on the Earth,
And she could only moan
In agony,
"O God, what has happened? Can you not help us?"
Silence.

Silence. Silence.
Then the silence was torn asunder by a moan
Deep and feral
It crawled up and out of her throat—a blood-curdling scream—
Her scream baptized her Dearborn in crimson grief.
She cradled him in her arms,
Observed a new opening in his head.
Pressed his lifeless, gaping mouth
To her empty breast.

He drew no sustenance.
His blood oozed from that other opening
Created with a club by his brother.
It filled her lap
And ran between her thighs
Like it did that painful morning he was born.
But there was no life there,
Only more pain than she could endure.
She wailed
As she embraced death.

And God's great heart was touched.
He heard her call
And remembered the pain
In his own heart
When his Dearborn
Would spill out his life
On the rocky ground.
And God's great mother-heart wept
At the plan he had conceived
That would comfort the woman
And all of her children
Yet to be.

Labyrinth

Good Friday
Around three o'clock Santa Fe time,
Coinciding more or less
With the time of Jesus' death,
Give or take a couple of millennia,
I began my solitary pilgrimage
On a winding path—a labyrinth—
In a courtyard on Museum Hill,
A cultured if not altogether holy place.
And it was the Holy for which I longed.
Friends accompanied me
On this contemplative hike,
Yet we were each alone for this brief pilgrimage
We were told.
For me, however, there was another pilgrim
Walking to my left and one step behind me
Like a like a familiar friend
Who cast no shadow.
"Trading one superstition for another?" he whispered.
I took the first step reverently,
The next steps methodically.
Even the steps were silent.
Walk, walk, step, walk, walk, step,
Turn, go back, turn again.
Each turn was like repentance,
Changing the direction in which I was headed.

A gray-haired fellow-walker was exiting

As I was entering,

Bringing us face to face.

He stopped and looked quizzically at me.

What shall we do at this impasse

Was the silent, implied question

Expressed by his raised eyebrows.

I stepped aside, smiled, and motioned him by with a nod.

He bowed deeply to me,

Pressing his hands together as though in prayer,

And passed on by.

"That is his attempt at ritual, that bowing-to-you moment,"

My shadowless friend said.

"Is this a holy moment for you?

An Asian greeting? Holy?" he sighed.

I was silent still,

But I listened intently

For some way to recognize real holiness

When counterfeit was what I was used to.

What could I do to discern the difference?

Then I remembered:

The Lord's Supper Table at Temple Baptist Church

With its carving of

This Do in Remembrance of Me.

Then I remembered:
The silver-plated plates filled with
Crumbled, salt-less, soda crackers
As holy as any Host elevated in any cathedral
In New York or Rome.

Then I remembered:
The stacks of trays holding
Little glasses of grape juice
As holy as ornate silver chalices of finest wines
In any church in Canterbury or Paris.

Then I remembered:
The sound of Mrs. Hayes' piano
During "Break Thou the Bread of Life"
As the small containers drained of their prosaic nectar
Clicked into their resting places
In the holders beside the hymnals,
A holy, happy, clicking percussion
For the musical offering.

The holy was there,
Always had been there.
It followed me to this wind-swept courtyard,
Wondering if superstition was
Merely another way of dealing
With mystery.
For me, it was not.
I found the holy in the mystery.

Santa Fe Afternoon

The wind plays the aspen trees
Like visual tambourines
Making the softest sound
As the ecstatic leaves
Still fresh
Shiver in anticipation
Of a gentle touch.
Then the entire tree seems to stretch and preen
As music is performed in the key of green.

New Mexican Monsoon

The rain like a shimmering, gauzy net
Filters the afternoon light.
Through a tightly woven weave
It softens the vibrant colors
To muted, silver-washed tones
Of the original hues.
The news is moist,
And the voice of the birds taking refuge
In the trees
Continues to sing
As life is renewed
In this freshly baptized valley.

From Whence Come the Gods

Oh, yes! It is easy to see the Gods
Incarnate in the clouds.
Huge mountainous beings slowly turning
With majestic, regal moves
As the grandeur of summer thunderstorms
Slowly waltzes across the azure ethers.
There, high and lifted up, is Jupiter
In all his regal Roman solemnity,
And Mercury dancing with wings on his feet,
And beautiful Apollo
Riding the sun like a chariot.

Surely, the bright, billowing forms
Touching the blue dome
Towering over mere mortals
Are eternal.
And so we name them to deify them,
Arrange them in a futile attempt at order,
And attribute intentions to them:
Shade, sunlight,
Water, wonder and delight
With rain falling
On the good and bad,
Young and old,
Living and dead,
Making life with wine and bread.

As we pray to the giant Gods we call everlasting,
We notice that they constantly change,
Never the same.
They become mere emissaries of the wind.
So our fickle hearts turn
To that invisible form that moves mountainous deities
To another valley
As though they were no more than fluffy sheep,
Leaving us to contemplate the word:
Mystery,
Wondering if there might be something
Directing the wind,
Something larger than the clouds,
The mountains,
The sky,
The mind.

The Psalms

The Psalms are so human to me that I can read them over and over and always find delight. There are times when I read them as though I were reading *lectio divina*, a contemplative way of praying. When one seeks inspiration from Scriptures, one reads a passage three times and waits to see what words stand out and seem to be speaking to oneself. The words that stand out are the message for the moment. While reading Psalms, this is often the experience I have, even if the message is not initially apparent. I have chosen a few psalms on which to meditate, and I have gleaned these thoughts from them.

A Clean Heart

"Create in me a clean heart, O God, and renew a right spirit within me."
Psalm 51:10

Lord,

I've been baptized,

Sanitized,

Etherized on a table—

To borrow from Mr. Elliott's verse.

In one way or another

I have been clean

For short periods of time.

But I keep slipping back

Into the slime,

A victim of the curse.

I want to be your

Perfect child.

But all the while

I think of things to do
That can be described
As wild.
With dirt and smudges
Around my heart,
I thank you for doing
Your holy, mysterious part
Of seeing me as clean
After being washed white as snow
In a crimson stream.
What does clean mean?
Perfect? Antiseptic?
Not human?
No bad smells or stains
Or grime under broken nails?
No lust or greed or envy?
No itching or vermin?
How can I ever be clean?
I live in a society built in Gehenna,
In a house of dung.
Is this how Cowper felt when he wrote
Of that gory fountain filled with blood
That cleanses?

Upright

". . . for praise is comely for the upright." Psalm 33:1

Don't get me wrong, Lord,

I understand what the scholars

Of King James meant

By upright.

But to me upright is an

Old piano in Grandma's

Front room

Laden with

Crocheted scarves,

Family photographs,

Dime store finery,

And plastic flowers.

Plus an old holy Broadman hymnal

Second only to the Holy Bible

As far as books are concerned.

We would gather around that out-of-tune

Instrument

And sing old songs to our old God

And our new God

Our first God

And our last God.

And the praise was as

Out of tune

As that old upright,

But in our hearts

It was a beautiful song
That angels longed to
Sing.

Calm the Waters, Lord

"Thou didst cleave the fountain and the flood: thou driedst up mighty rivers."
Psalm 74:15

Standing on the shores of a
Mountain lake,
I remembered how you parted the water.
Then I remembered the other time
You calmed the sea:
Soft day colored gray
Hovered quietly in the air.
Evening mist gently kissed
The lake reflecting there.
Wave's colors brushed the shores
Like the hem of Joseph's coat.
Wind softly reminded me of
A baby in bulrushes—
Innocent afloat.

Sleeping like a child
On his mother's breast
In the bow of a fishing boat
He took a fleeting rest.
Storms erupted round him
And terrified the men.
He slowly opened up his eyes
And he began to grin.
He held his hands up to the sky

And then he laughed out loud.
He shook his hair in the wind
And kissed a playful cloud
Then knelt him down
To touch the sea.
The men screamed out in fear.
"Don't be afraid," he said,
"Remember, I am here."
And to the sea he said,
"I've slept,
You rocked me like a child,
And I dreamed a dream—a peaceful dream—for a little while.
I was a babe and I could hear
Mary's heartbeat very near.
You, Galilee, have done my will,
Now, Galilee, peace. Peace be still."

Liturgy

". . . His praise shall continually be in my mouth." Psalm 34:1

I remember your advice, Lord,

About vain repetitions.

And I try to praise you

In fresh, new ways . . .

In honest ways.

You alone know our hearts

And the shape they are in.

You alone see me flinch.

You alone know my petty sin

That comes from my own pride,

But I can't hide my chagrin

At all those "Praise the Lorders"

Who come marching in to vex

My spirit.

Repetition's redundant echo

Is their hollow praise;

Why can they not hear it?

Can't they see the vacant look

As their own eyes glaze

Over?

Pavlov's own Rover

Could not act more on cue.

Is all this constant commotion

What you are due?

Now far be it from me to judge;

But I have my principles
And from them, I'll not budge.
I think a reverent hallelujah
On every third Sunday should do ya.

Show Us God

"And hide not thy face from thy servant." Psalm 69:17

Lord, I prayed,

Like James and John I long to see your face.

Is it glowing white or shimmering gold?

Eternal light, ageless yet old?

Do you hang suspended like

Michelangelo's muscled God

Pointing fingers to clay figurines

In semi-recumbent postures?

It seems odd.

Do you flutter a faultless dove

Descending from above cooing about:

Father, Son, and Holy Ghost and love?

Would you turn my hair white

If I saw your glorious light?

That's the way Cecil B. depicted

Moses in his movie loosely based on

Your book.

Can I please have a look?

Then I heard you whisper:

"Child,

You cannot look upon my face,

But I will show you what I have shown

The whole human race.

I will show you instead my innermost part

My only begotten son, my Jesus, my heart."

Dominion?

"Thou madest him to have dominion over the works of thy hands; thou hast put all things under his feet." Psalm 8:6

Lord, ever since the
Garden of Eden
Things have gone down.
The weeds have grown wild,
And thorns have torn holes
In the prophet's robes.
Men have used your
Exquisite earth
In a perverted way.
Digging in its bowels
To burn dead dinosaurs
To foul the air.
We have not played fair.
And we don't seem to care
That you expect us to be accountable,
Having put all things under our domain.
So we use them
As a mere muddy-boot
Cleaning device.

Autumnal Days

"Cast me not off in the time of old age; forsake me not when my strength faileth." Psalm 71:9

Lord, I've seen them in a *home*
In activity groups, yet alone.
Their fingers bent around their canes
And shoulders stooped by various pains,
Many reading and rereading the
Promises they can claim
In your book.

Lord, it was not you that cast them off
Like old, faded, wrinkled clothes
With seams weakened, frayed sleeves, and a patch
Here and there that shows.
We did it, Lord,
For a variety of reasons.
Unlike you,
We only enjoy the youthful seasons of spring
Where birds sing and insects buzz
And trees dance in gowns of dazzling green.
We ignore the old in robes of gold
Doing their stately dance.
Trees that sway on a late
November day
Never seem to say what we want to hear
About youth, gaiety, and cheer.

Wisdom is simple
As a bare winter branch
Against the snows,
A gnarled hand opened
To share the things it knows.

Prayer

In order to pray
I obey the one who taught us to say, "Our Father . . . "
I enter my closet,
Close my eyes,
Bow my head,
And in the darkness I listen.
Shhhh.
Only silence,
And stillness and waiting,
Until finally I hear the metered rush of my pulse
Like the syncopated sound of a meandering pedestrian
Walking through brittle autumn leaves
In rhythm to a heart's beat,
Yours or mine, I can't tell.
Is it you coming again in the cool of the evening?

I am still,
Chin resting on my chest,
Listening.
Listening.
Listening
For the words.
Please, speak to me.
Are you here?
Near?
Are you in the dark?

There is no spark,

No glimmer, no shimmer, no candle, no star,

No dazzling reflection,

No light in the closet with my eyes closed.

Science tells me that:

Everything was reduced

To a pinpoint of energy

Which suddenly exploded!

Bang!

Big bang!

And everything that is appeared,

Hurled forth effortlessly,

Meeting no resistance,

Sliding, whirling, flying

Across the vast expanse of nothingness.

Who or what harvested that pre-explosion energy into bundles

Of vibrating sheaves?

What was reduced to that infinitesimally small finite mass, and from

whence?

What was in the void?

Was it only the dark?

And darkness? Is not darkness something?

Matter?

Energy?

What was before the explosion, God?

Darkness?

Is God dark?

And all those cataclysmic conflagrations
Throwing light across emptiness
In dazzling arrays of randomness,
Jewels displayed against black velvet,
Is that mere ornamentation?
Are you the darkness from which we all sprang?
Is that why I find you in my closet
When my eyes are closed
In the silence?

Need I not fear the dark
Because that is who you are, too?
Mystery creating out of a need to do,
Making doing, good
By virtue of the fact that you alone are doing.
Is all that is Good?
Are you all goodness?
And am I included in that goodness?
Is this how I find you in this lovely, desperate search?
Go to the dark, the silence, and listen?
Do I hear you walking toward me
Across the scattered days of my life,
Strewn across the landscape of my existence,
Sounding like a meandering pedestrian
Walking through brittle, autumn leaves?
The rhythm of a heart's beat
Yours or mine,
I can't tell,
Here in the cool of the evening.

The Bread of Life

Hunger.
For food?
No, more.
Hunger for life.
Bread allows you to live.
It nourishes via
Sun, minerals in dirt
Transformed into plants
Harvested, husked, winnowed,
Ground, baked, ingested, eliminated.
Bread, the staff of life,
Is the thing for which you hunger,
You think.
"I am the bread of life," he said.
It is a metaphor, the divine kind.
Bread sustains life, so it is life for which you really hunger,
Not sunlight and dirt metamorphosed into carbohydrates.
God is the source of all life,
So it is God for whom you hunger.
He is Life.
Life is what He is and what He gives.
Take, eat, observe, participate and remember
That you are a part of life,
That you are a part of God,
That it is good.
To hunger for food?

No, more.

Hunger for life,

And know that you are living.

When Paradise

There is somewhere I want to be,
Somewhere exotic and far away
Where mountains like pillars of eternal granite
Support the fragile, lapis lazuli dome called sky,
Where people have a different look in their eye,
An open look with mouths agape
And their hearts loving
Because that is what hearts do,
And beat, and ache.
Where the air smells sweet and clean,
Conveying secrets
About angels and incense,
Terrifying holiness,
Unconditional acceptance,
And permission to drink the thick, rich essence of life
Until I shudder satiated,
Then I sing like a drunk
With joy unleashed.
I want to dance
Unabashedly,
Twisting and twirling,
Expanding and contracting
Like Isadora Duncan
Amongst the Parthenon's ancient marble columns,
Or like Pachacutec,
The Inca king running barefoot

Through the high, wind-swept streets of Machu Picchu
Dressed only in a golden mask,
Dazzling feathers,
And caressing clouds,
Golden skin longing to be touched,
Dancing with palms turned upward
Cupping life like a red passion,
A living flame
Offered back to the mysterious maker
Who created oceans of options,
Promising glorious kingdoms
Just across that ample,
Barely explored,
Mostly uncharted ocean
Called Life.

Souvenir

I see you,

An entire shop of yous.

You are not life-like,

Not skillfully carved,

Nor realistic

With eyes accurately, anatomically rendered

Looking heavenward,

Graceful feet artfully arranged,

Loincloth carefully draped.

Instead, feet are stacked one on the other to economize on nails,

Fingers not delicately displayed,

No, splayed.

You are roughhewn,

Quickly carved to be

Efficiently dispersed to an ambling crowd of customers

Meandering between the narrow, heavy-laden aisles.

You are no more than a hastily constructed religious artifact for purchase.

Commerce is the reason you are hanging there in rows.

No one knows

That I stand here dazed

My mind in a haze

As I see what capitalism has done to you.

I see you,

An entire shop of only you hanging

Head tilted,

Knees bent,

Strength spent,

Blood spilt

In a primitive attempt

To represent

A sacrifice to a God

Who is placated by blood,

Innocent blood.

The horror called holiness sends shivers,

And I realize that this is Now,

Not the Past or Tomorrow,

But Now awash in sorrow,

And I see you lined in neat rows

Cruciform, after cruciform, after cruciform—

Now.

Does she Now kneel on the rocks

At the base of the cross?

Is she still saying yes to the request

She bear the Son of God?

Is she in birth pangs Now?

Is Now the core of God's eternal will?

And resurrection—

Is he rising Now from the grave?

And am I Now and Again and Forever a ten-year-old boy

At Temple Baptist Church

Weeping in my pew, praying,

"Jesus, make me new.

Save me Now."

I leave the souvenir shop
With no purchase in my hand,
Stumbling like a man
Drunk on new wine,
Fleeing Now,
Running toward any other manifestation of Time.
Jesus, are you still in the Now?
Is that crown still on your brow?
Is your mother still drowning in all that sorrow?
Jesus Christ! I can't stand this.
Meet me at Tomorrow.
Was that a futile prayer?
Are you already there?
Is Now what creates tomorrow?
Is Now all there is,
Has there only been Now?
Is there no time
That we can define as Past or Future?
Is this what scripture refers to when I read:
"Behold the Lamb, slain from the Foundation of the world"?
Always slain?
Does he hang on that cross for as long as Now is?
Is he Now screaming out his great lament?
Do his tortured words cause God to repent
This convoluted path toward salvation?
Is that awful cry his final oblation
As the ultimate question is sent Godward,
"Why? . . . Why? . . . Why

Have you forsaken me?"
And the veil of the Temple is rent
Top to bottom, heaven to earth,
Revealing in the Now that the Holy of Holies
Holds no mystery
And reveals nothing.
No thing. No. Thing.
Jesus, you are alone Now,
No family,
No mother,
No religion,
Abandoned by even God.
I scream out, "This cannot be!
Can you not feel me?
Is not my Now as real as yours?"

My mind is racing, clouded with dark doubt.
What is all this religion about anyway?
Where are my thoughts going?
Why can I not see what I want to say?
In this chaos of not knowing,
Something is pressed against me.
I can't see, so I feel
Another construction of wood,
A ladder.
Leaning against the only other object standing,
Your cross,
Slowly, fearfully, I climb

Lest a sudden movement

Cause you more pain.

I mount the ladder

Propped against the back of the cross.

Do you feel me slowly climbing upward?

I am here, Now.

Can you feel my arms encircle you

And the rough wood to which you are nailed?

Can you feel me brush

The blood, tears, and hair from your eyes?

Shoo the flies?

Can you feel my pounding heart

Soundly syncopated with yours?

As sobbing chokes my voice,

Hear my heart praying:

"I love you. I always have.

I always will.

I love you, Now.

"Who is there?" you ask.

"I AM," I say

In a voice that sounds like a moan,

Reminding you and me

That we are not alone.

Never have been.

World without end.

Amen and Amen and Amen.

With Thanks to Rilke

I sit in silence—
Praying?
Meditating?
Thinking about You
And your silence
In the silence.
I listen, longing
To hear your message,
But hear only more silence.

Eventually, I become aware of something—
A sound? No, two sounds
Found in me.
High and sharp, piercing like energy,
And low like heavy wheels rumbling on train tracks
Carrying rusty iron ore.

Was the silence broken by me and transported
Over a nervous and circulatory system
Delivering energy and red, body-rejuvenating blood,
Or was it broken by you
As you send a coded word?
It falls to the floor
Tapping out messages
Like raindrops in a pool,
Like horses' hooves on a road,

Like trumpet fanfares encompassing the walls of Jericho
Revealing that you are,
And I join you
Making harmony in the Symphony of Creation
Destroying barriers,
Making music
Composed of
Sound and Silence.

Take, Eat

When I broke free of the chrysalis
Stretched my newly formed wings and soared
Around you
I thought to reveal a delicate Monarch design
Patterned like fragile stained-glass windows
Hoping to imitate holiness
Or royalty.
Neither.

I am a mere moth,
Thick of body and dusty of wing.
Still it is you I long to be near, to touch.
With no voice, yet I long to sing.
Instead, I begin to eat holes
In the seamless, white woolen robe
Carefully woven from the fleece
Of a lamb without spot or blemish
As a testament to my hunger.
I leave destruction,
Little moth-eaten holes.
I fight to rise from
The hem of your garment
To your face,
A great distance for me.
I grow weak as I begin to fiercely flutter
Feeling as though I am falling

When I sense a rushing of a mighty wind
As you bend low,
And with a gentle swoop
Catch me in your hand.
My insect form is brought up level to your eyes
Where I see
Opening for me
Nothing less than Paradise.

Star Stuff

Over half a century ago
We were kids camped out in the backyard.
Pillows and Mama's blankets did not camouflage the fact that
The earth was still hard.
Our gaze was skyward.
Stars were more visible then.
We had returned from Sunday evening services
After hearing about a fire-and-brimstone future again
The result of our wicked, childhood sin.
The sermon all but deprived us of hope,
And that night,
Lying on your back
You let go of that rope,
And dared to fall into the depths of despair
As you wondered if it really mattered
If God even cared.
"What if earth is just a speck on God's turd,
And He's already flushed the toilet?"
I'll never forget that profound word.

Years passed.
My life lived to three score and ten.
Yet still I hear your adolescent voice
Making its choice,
And marvel at your juvenile wit
When you snickered, "Holy shit."

Were you a pessimist abandoning hope,
Or merely a realist who made
Theology and philosophy a joke?
I can't say.
I still wonder today.

Your query helped me in my quest
To see life in a more optimistic way.
I am—we are—passing passengers
On this speck of dirt
Rotating around a lesser star.
But we are, Kenny. We are!

Whether we are eternal
Or gone with a flush,
We continue in this vortex.
I believe at least this much:
We are made of the stuff
That comes from God:
Brown clay,
Brown shit,
Brown, brittle lotus pods.
Now hear me, Kenny—
Gone like a bolt from the blue—
I still hear you,
And I am glad that we were there
And we still are . . .
Made of the stuff
Of every other star.

The Bride of Christ

Poor, vulnerable bride,

Barely ambulatory

With your gown in tatters,

You stagger down an endless aisle to the ancient altar

Your face covered by a smothering veil.

Why do you come to your wedding besmirched and bruised?

Who has done this to you?

"Who, indeed!" you wail.

When the betrothal was first announced,

We gathered around like a frolicking flock of frisky lambs.

As you ran in rapture through the fields of lilies,

Pollen streaked your dress like instantly embroidered yellow happiness

On your billowing skirt.

Morning mist softly veiled your dazzling innocence.

Carrying a bouquet of Rose-of-Sharon

As though you were waving a happy trophy,

Laughter rose from your delicate throat like music.

The grace of the arch of your satin slipper peeked from under your silk

hem

Inspired the dead to dance.

The bounce of the curls cascading down your back

Motivated hallelujahs from the chorus of children dancing behind you.

As you ran toward your Lover

Heart filled with exquisite joy,

Your eyes suddenly widened with horror at what you saw.

He hung there
Clothed not in wedding finery,
Rather in sweat and blood.
Vital fluids flowed from the crown of his head,
Anointed him with gore,
Slowly flowed down his side
Dripped from the tips of his toes to the hard, parched earth.
Your mouth formed a silent scream.
You fell to your knees clutching the cruel cross
To your heaving, grieving heart
Where the crimson stains on your virginal white dress
Formed Rorschach ink blots of brutality
All too easy to interpret.

In sorrow he looked down from his tower
Knowing that your eternal sacred bond condemned you
To the weeping wounds of certain crucifixion, too.
Poor battered bride of Christ.
Tatterdemalion in soiled peau de soie.

Meditations

Ideas swarm

Buzzing in my mind.

Are they demon's legions

Or hordes of Heavenly Host

Encircling me like gnats

I swat,

Then splat!

None dies

Each multiplies

And the sound becomes guttural,

Then choral

As they harmonize on a lost chord

That speaks beyond primitive concepts of

Our Lord.

I am consumed by a holy flame

As the Cosmos sings aloud

The beauty of your eternal name.

Dawn at Madeline's

The leaves turn imperceptibly in acknowledgment
As the hills to the east bow
At the arrival of the glorious Apollo,
His chariot of gold transporting him over amethyst heavens,
His hair aflame flowing
As he sows the dark path of night
Spreading light before him like iridescent waves
Delighting himself at the kaleidoscopic revelations
Of an awakening world.

And I drink my coffee
And listen
And watch
And wait as the day begins
Reminding myself that night ultimately ends.
And light dances.

Fired Clay Cup

Fired clay cup curving, insulated in my encircling hands
Tangible, tactile, authentic
Molded by a potter to be utilitarian
Perhaps beautiful
If form meets function efficiently.

I envy the potter with dirty hands
Who makes cups, pots, and plates.
I have no such pragmatic gift.
I grasp at thoughts that may become ideas
Trying to mold them into words, then phrases, then sentences
No more substantial than:
A mist rising in the morning,
A silk scarf of an idea whirled around by
A Ghost dancer gliding across an empty stage
In an abandoned theatre,
Ephemeral thoughts,
Mere air.

Is there a market for air in this world?
Can it be realized?
Must it be sanitized, pasteurized and
Packaged and labeled
In order to be served at the supper table?
Or can it be held simply
Like this fired clay cup curving, insulated in my encircling hands?

Addendum:
A Little Child Shall Lead Them

I did not want to climb a mountain. I never like to work up a sweat after my morning shower, but here we were in Estes Park, Colorado, and my wife felt a good mountain climb would be quality family time. Of course, that kind of tugging at paternal heartstrings plays a quiet pizzicato, and I always respond to that kind of music. So, off we started into the woods for a walk: Mamma Bear, Papa Bear, Boy Bear, and pretty little pink Girl Bear. To put this outing in a more literal setting, I must name the characters involved as me, my wife Cynthia, my seven-year-old son Will, and my five-year-old daughter Lily. And, of course, as my daughter is ever thoughtful to point out, God was with us too. This last member of the hiking party I thanked profusely when I saw the tram at the base of the mountain that would haul us to the top, eliminating an exhausting hike.

The ride up was exhilarating as we floated effortlessly over the tops of the evergreens. The children stood on tiptoe, peering out the window of the little red carriage that seemed to float to the mountaintop. After a solid thud and a strong, safe-sounding click, the tram was stopped. As we stepped out, we were greeted by a horde of hungry chipmunks. For an astronomical price, we purchased two small bags of peanuts and watched the children delight in these seemingly tame creatures. All too soon the peanuts were gone, and chipmunks with distended cheeks that would rival Dizzy Gillespie's seemed satisfied. Not so the children.

"Please, buy some more peanuts, Daddy," they begged.

"No. Don't you understand, children? When you teach these wild animals to depend on you for food, they stop depending on themselves. They then lose the ability to fend for themselves out here in this wilderness. And when the tourists stop coming, the poor chipmunks would be so lazy and so fat, they could not find food for themselves or their *babies* and they would starve," I wisely said, knowing the implied danger to babies would touch Lily's tender heart, and they would stop begging me for money. However, Lily folded her expressive hands into the universal sign of supplication, knelt in the dirt among the peanut shells, and prayed, "Please, Daddy."

So much for lessons in survival in the wilds of Colorado. So much for consistency in parenting. I bought the peanuts and watched with delight as my children fed the obese rodents. Lily, ever concerned for the smaller animals, guarded her bag of peanuts and fed them to only the smaller, shyer chipmunks. Will was exuberant and excessive in throwing his peanuts to all of them. The larger, more aggressive chipmunks got the larger portion, and he was soon out of nuts. Lily was still savoring the elations of tenderly feeding the more needy rodents. (Long after Will has gulped down his ice cream cone, or cookie, or pie, or what-have-you, Lily is lingering over her treat.)

"Come on, Dad! Let's go." Will tugged impatiently at my hand.

"You boys go on ahead," Cynthia said. "I'll stay here with Mother Teresa and we'll catch up with you in a bit."

We followed the path as it went past a huge bolder, took a sharp turn to reveal a breath-taking vista. Will and I paused for a moment and drank in the scene, when suddenly he started off up the steep trail. We were exhilarated, and we both felt the urge to climb higher and higher. The higher we climbed, the narrower the trail became, and with a few more turns and twists we found ourselves standing on the edge of a very high cliff. The up-rush of the wind blew our hair and cooled our sweaty backs. We walked to the edge and peered over.

I sat down on the rocky cliff and Will sat beside me. I wanted him closer. I wanted my arms around him, and not just for his safety. I was so happy, so full of wonder and joy, that I wanted to share that feeling with him. I scooted back and Will sat between my legs, leaving two sets of feet dangling over the precipice. My arms encircled his chest and felt his little seven-year-old heart beating rapidly with the climb, the altitude, and the excitement of perching on the edge of the world. This experience stirred me to the center of my soul. It was a transcendent moment—beyond tears, beyond words. Will and I sat there listening to the rush of the mountain wind. If we leaned over and peered down to the bottom of the cliff, we could feel the force of the strong wind blowing in our faces. It seemed then that we could have hurled ourselves out into the strong upward drafts and been borne upward like Icarus and Daedalus and soared until we touched the golden face of the sun.

Before us, across the valley, was the high ridge of powerful mountains. They stood with solid, stone hearts impervious to storms, snows, even time it seemed. The mountains seemed eternal in their grandeur and majesty. I then thought of the ancient Hebrews looking up at Mt. Sinai after they had spent so many years in the flat delta of the Nile basin. How awesome the mountain must have looked to their eyes. I could see how they would have thought that God lived in that mountain. I certainly could envision God living in those mountains with such divine attributes. It was then I realized that the deity was addressing me. There was no audible voice, only the sound of the wind and an occasional screech of a soaring hawk. But God communicated with me. I would call this experience a theophany.

"You see those mountains? Eloquent. I overemphasized wrinkles in the earth's surface, that's all. I create the mountains, but that's not who I am," God said.

The clear blue sky was speckled with a herd of fleecy white clouds that seemed to hurry past the mountains, causing cloud shadows to make the scene variegated with cool then bright greens and blues and tans. My eyes looked to the source of the shadows, the light. The sun was as yellow as a yellow circle Lily would have painted in her primary blue sky. It was warm, life giving, and beautiful to behold. I understood how people down through the ages had been led to worship the sun. Again God spoke to me.

"It is lovely, my sun. It is excessive in its life-sustaining abilities, but it is only one of my smaller stars. I created it with prodigal exuberance. The sun is godlike, but that is not who I am."

Sprawling out before Will and me was the valley with shimmering ribbons of water cascading into a glowing sapphire lake. I knew the valley was teeming with life, not only wild creatures that nervously survived in the ever-growing population of year-round residence, but also families of tourists like us. People. The valley was filled to the brim with people. People recreating and procreating. People laughing and worrying. Good people, bad people. Sick people, well people. Sad people, happy people. People of every shade of color and faith, and nation, and tongue. People. The tenders of the garden. Once more God spoke to me.

"I am the creator of all you see, but I am that which is also invisible. All you are able to perceive is something I created with just a thought."

I rested my chin on the top of Will's blond head and hugged him tighter. I felt his little arms respond to my arms with a tighter hold. At my close proximity to my son, my senses were full of him. His warm, compact, little seven-year-old body pressed to me, the smell of his sweaty hair not unlike the smell of puppies, the dazzling golden color of his hair that was so close to my eyes that I could not focus clearly and saw only shimmering gold, a crown of golden light transfiguring my son into a king or a heavenly being. My heart was so full of love for him that I thought the joy would surely overwhelm me. Tears filled my eyes.

Then I saw the tree. I was not more than five or six feet away, and it was not like the towering pines that grew in the valley. It was a poor, distant relation with a twisted trunk, gnarled limbs, and short, pointed needles. Somehow it looked ancient, even biblical; there on that mountain, my arms around my firstborn, I thought of Father Abraham and his son Isaac.

"Go to the mountain and offer your son, Isaac, as a sacrifice to me," the voice said inside that old head.

And he obeyed! How could he do that? How could his old legs, weary from years of migrant moving, propel him up the mountain? How could his ancient heart that pumped faithfully for over a hundred years sustain him? Why did no tears blind his rheumy eyes as he watched his joy skip up the mountain like a spring kid? How could he find the strength to pile stone upon stone, kindling upon kindling? What kept him from grabbing Isaac's hand and plunging headlong off the mountain to escape the terrible command of this invisible God who had always kept covenants, but was now so easily about to break one?

Abraham, Abraham, how could you have obeyed that God?

And it seemed to me the gnarled evergreen close to me and Will was changed into a ram. At least, in a twisted limb I could make out the shape of a curled ram's horn. And the veil of tears in my eyes blurred the scene so that the tree once more changed, and I saw another more terrible shape—a cruciform. No ram this time, instead a lamb.

"God so loved the world that he gave his only begotten son that whosoever believes on him shall not perish but have everlasting life."

And God spoke to me.

"You see the mountains? I created them, but that is not who I am. You see the sun? I created it, but that is not who I am. You see the valley? I created it, but that is not who I am. I will reveal myself to you like I did to Moses and Abraham and all those who had eyes to see me."

I waited, but not for long.

"You know that feeling you have for Will and he has for you?

"Yes," I answered.

"A feeling so real that it is almost tangible?"

"Yes."

"Well, the thing that binds your heart to his; that is who I am."

"Dear God . . . "

"Yes, I Am *that* I Am. And the love you feel for Will is something like the love I feel for everything I have created. Take the love you feel for your child and multiply it times God. That is how I feel for all my creation."

And the vision ended, and I began to weep. Will turned and looked into my face questioningly, but he never said a word. We got up to go and heard what sounded like music. It was Cynthia and Lily even higher up the mountain than we had been, and they were waving, laughing and calling us on.

www.ingramcontent.com/pod-product-compliance
Lightning Source LLC
Chambersburg PA
CBHW061733050726
47598CB00002B/464